Leadership

How Effective Leaders Construct A High-performance Culture Of Accountability And Responsibility Is The Subject Of The Book "Accountability Leadership."

(The Ability To Motivate And Influence Those Around You Is An Essential Component Of Leadership)

Forrest Nolan

TABLE OF CONTENT

What Is The Precise Delineation Of Success?.....1

Your Reliance On Your Team Supersedes Their Reliance On You. 7

How To Demonstrate Professionalism And Foster Positive Relationships With An Unfavorable Coworker To Effectively Advance In The Workplace 37

Fostering Loyalty...........56

How Can They Establish Connections With Others?...........76

Developing Your Team...........119

The Leadership Of Innovation...........129

The Leader Of The Organized Group...........158

What Is The Precise Delineation Of Success?

Certain individuals define success based on the sense of equilibrium they achieve between their professional lives and the other aspects of their lives. For those individuals, work does not constitute the essence of accomplishment. They acknowledge the necessity of adapting one's life and recognize that work should not hold primacy in our lives. John Woolman, a pioneering advocate against slavery during the early years of America, virtually ceased his occupation as a tailor due to the imperative necessity of emancipating himself from the burdensome weight of stress. When the equilibrium of his work became disrupted, exerting control over him and leaving him with little time for other meaningful pursuits, he did not perceive himself as being productive. If an occupation consumes someone's life, commanding their entire attention and leaving no room for a harmonious balance between work, physical exercise, familial and social connections, and spiritual growth, then it is widely regarded as unhealthy and unsuccessful. This can give rise to a hectic lifestyle, as well as physical ailments, interpersonal conflicts, and neglect of the principles that contribute to a fulfilling life.

In the end, many individuals define success based on the evaluation of their life's legacy upon their eventual demise. Will individuals who are actively participating engage in discussions regarding the individual's financial earnings, or possibly even express their disappointment in the person using the phrase "no love lost"? Furthermore, will they be engaging in a discussion about this individual's current obligations and their sense of privilege in referring to this person as a friend or colleague? For the majority, success is ultimately defined by the positive impact that has been made and the lasting legacy associated with the accomplishments of an individual. Has the person exerted a beneficial influence on the global sphere?

You may be familiar with the proverb: success is a voyage, not a destination. I agree, on the whole. The pursuit holds greater enjoyment than the attainment. We deeply value the excitement of the endeavor, the vitality of the forthcoming events, the possibilities that lie within them, and the confidence that accompanies such moments. Once you have achieved your goals, it is imperative to establish a range of objectives in order to experience that sense of excitement once more.

Many individuals mistakenly believe that success is intertwined with material possessions. However, the truth is that success is determined by one's self-perception and the ability to derive fulfillment from one's life. In order to lead a fully productive and fulfilling life, it is imperative to acknowledge and delve into the following four fundamental principles, which are extensively discussed within the confines of this discourse. Prior to delving into those, let us first discuss some considerations.

People from various regions are constantly seeking profound tranquility. I define substantial tranquility as liberation from fear, anxiety, discontent, and culpability. I believe that we strive for profound tranquility through various avenues, some of which may be detrimental while others prove to be beneficial. Certain individuals seek genuine tranquility through self-assurance, some through financial stability, some through their interpersonal connections, others through their professional endeavors, and yet some resort to seeking solace in dependencies such as substance abuse or gambling in an attempt to fill this profound emptiness. However, only a limited few truly attain a state of tranquility beyond the bounds of their religious beliefs. Success, irrespective of its nature, requires a profound sense of tranquility; otherwise, your prosperity will be lackluster and diluted.

True accomplishment cannot truly be defined without the presence of excellent physical and mental health, as well as the energy to fully savor and embrace life. Without these essential components, what may appear as achievement is merely a superficial and incomplete version of what it has the potential to be. A considerable number of financially prosperous individuals employ their wealth in ambitious endeavors aimed at restoring their well-being or maintaining their vitality and vigor. An achievement devoid of wellness and vitality resembles a high-end automobile lacking fuel. As is commonly proclaimed globally, these individuals are "full of sound and fury, signifying nothing."

Irrespective of the extent of one's financial success, it remains a hollow experience if there is no one with whom to share it. It is not strictly limited to a spouse or partner; individuals such as parents, children, companions, or other relatives can also fulfill this role. It is important to bear in mind that Scrooge was financially prosperous; however, he lacked inner tranquility and lacked any companionship with whom to share it. His prosperity was vacant.

Your Reliance On Your Team Supersedes Their Reliance On You.

Leaders are remunerated for the collective achievements, regardless of their positive or negative outcomes, of our team. The failure of the team reflects upon our leadership. It is the responsibility of leaders to mitigate obstacles and impediments in order to ensure the team's triumph. The team's success serves as our standard of measurement. Please take into account the challenges that are impeding the progress of the team. Analyze potential remedies to the impediments and devise strategies for their elimination.

Numerous managers commence their professional journeys with a mindset characterized by an authoritative disposition wherein subordinates are expected to comply obediently with directives. The majority of leaders commence with this approach, which is comprehensible. You will soon realize that the autocratic leadership style will significantly hinder your capacity to lead and wield effective influence.

Exhibit genuine sincerity and integrity when expressing your inspiration to colleagues; prioritize attentiveness, show genuine interest in their perspectives, and limit self-centric discussions. Utilize your emotional intelligence to comprehend their perspectives and effectively regulate your own emotions.

Ensuring openness and integrity are crucial aspects in earning an individual's trust. One of the greatest oversights that a leader can make is failing to acknowledge their mistakes. Integrity is exemplified by acknowledging one's shortcomings. While it is true that every leader aspires to achieve success, an integral aspect of exceptional leadership lies in the ability to embrace risks and maintain a willingness to confront failure. It is crucial to endeavour both failure and success. Acknowledging when something did not go according to plan is an integral aspect of exhibiting honesty to the team.

Exhibiting integrity and cultivating trust will enhance your capacity for impactful leadership. Refrain from engaging in the practice of attributing blame, and instead take responsibility for one's own shortcomings. The error will also present an occasion to learn effective strategies for navigating through setbacks. Formulating a strategic course of action to address the error, and effectively transform it into a catalyst for achievement.

In the subsequent chapters, you will discover that the acquisition of leadership skills and abilities is crucial for effectively fulfilling any leadership position. Leaders employ the capacity to exert influence in order to attain desired outcomes. Leaders provide individuals with the authority and autonomy to achieve their goals, while also eliminating obstacles that hinder their progress. Leaders exhibit unwavering determination, embrace accountability, and cultivate their abilities.

In order to effectively guide a formidable team and attain superior leadership, it is imperative that we adopt a mindset focused on continuous growth. We commence by regarding our employees and organizational partners as valued members of our team. Our personnel are regarded as team members rather than subordinates. Our primary association is that of partners. Our objective does not include exerting control over another individual. Our objective as leaders is to effectively lead, motivate, and provide guidance to others through the power of influence. The initiation of influence hinges upon comprehending our leadership approach and the individuals comprising our team.

8

The Existence of a Culture: Is It Appropriate?

Upon perusing several narratives within this literary compendium and devoting a considerable amount of contemplation to the imparted teachings, it becomes readily apparent that the veracity lies in the notion that individuals seldom emerge as the primary source of predicaments. The corollary to this assertion posits that triumph is cultivated through collaboration and not as a consequence of avoiding cooperation.

Throughout my professional tenure, I have consistently strived to uphold what I refer to as my "foundational principles of leadership," making a conscious effort to avoid the presumption that I consistently meet my own set standards. I have actively sought and received valuable input regarding the extent to which I am adhering steadfastly to those principles.

As a reader of this book, you are also encouraged to evaluate my adherence to the core tenets of leadership that I deeply value. In the titled 'Leadership Foundations' in the second section of this book, I will delve into an extensive dialogue regarding these foundational aspects and their potential implications for you. Currently, it is important to understand that the five principles that form the foundation of my leadership approach are as follows:

Actions and decisions carry the same weight as words, forming the foundation of trust in relationships (The trust equation).

Honesty is Non-Negotiable

Feedback serves as a Vital Instrument (For both reception and provision)

Every person aspires to achieve success.

The Ideas Are Here

Exemplifying strong leadership in the perspective of those whom I have supervised holds great significance to me. Upon receiving the following unsolicited feedback from one of my employees who was leaving to pursue a new opportunity and enhance their professional trajectory, I was particularly appreciative. Tara, who introduced herself, expressed the following sentiment: "Carson, you have effectively guided our organization by instilling a sense of inspiration within us, rather than resorting to coercion to drive us forward." This feedback, much like all the feedback we receive, was graciously regarded as a valuable contribution. Upon careful consideration of Tara's perceptive observation and sincere compliment, which I deemed to be wholly authentic coming from someone on their way out, devoid of any ulterior motives to boost the boss's ego, I found myself compelled to contemplate the true essence and implications of her words.

How does the act of kindling a fervent passion within an individual manifest itself?

How can an individual induce another individual to surpass their personal boundaries?

How can a leader assume accountability for the key drivers of success within the organization, thereby securing the commitment of the individuals comprising the workforce?

By what means can a leader unleash the notions and ingenuity concealed within the intellects and backgrounds of individuals within the organization?

The responses to the aforementioned inquiries are evidently diverse and boundless; nonetheless, there exist several straightforward factors that are pivotal in fashioning the culture of an enterprise into a driving force for corporate triumph. Essentially, every individual desires to excel and receive acknowledgment for their contributions. Individuals also desire to have their perspectives acknowledged and actively considered, rather than merely passively acknowledged. These two key determinants of success necessitate a leader to exhibit authenticity and wholeheartedly invest substantial time and effort into the organization. Based on my observations, the prevailing culture within the organization is well-founded and serves a purpose, even if it may not be acknowledged by past or present management. The factual truth concerning culture is that a distinct one exists, whether it be advantageous or disadvantageous. The inquiry at hand pertains to whether the culture aligns with your desired specifications and if it satisfies the essential requirements for the success of the business. A pondered examination of the present is indispensable for the attainment of an auspicious future outcome. In order to comprehend the existing culture effectively, and subsequently devise a strategy and plan to accommodate, modify, or enhance it, it is imperative that leaders initially assess and comprehend the underlying factors contributing to the establishment of the prevailing culture.

THE FIRE PIT

Anticipatability and the Aroma of Superior Cigars

The ability to make sound decisions is indispensable at all tiers.

—Peter Drucker

The premises featured a multitude of fire pits dispersed throughout. The most significant one was situated next to the primary bar connected to the lobby; it embodied a circular formation crafted from brown and ash sandstone, measuring approximately three feet in height and ten feet in diameter. The stone was enveloped by a polished rim made of concrete, exhibiting a light-gray hue. During the pleasant twilight hours, the gas fire pit offered a delightful scene, adorned with its expansive charcoal-colored tumbled lava stones. Approximately twelve sizable rattan chairs accompanied by red cushions encircled the central space, conveniently paired with individual side tables.

Ryan walked towards the pit in search of a pair of unoccupied seats positioned adjacently. As he advanced towards a pair of seats in close proximity to the pit, he perceived the voice of Tom resonating loudly from the vicinity of the bar, beckoning him: "Ryan, join me over here."

Ryan approached Tom, wearing a pleasant smile on his face. Hello again!

Tom gestured with the two cigars in his possession in an effort to capture Ryan's attention. Have you ever engaged in smoking? he asked.

I occasionally derive pleasure from indulging in a cigar.

Tom claimed to have taken an interest in cigars later in his adult years. I prefer to partake in their consumption once or twice on a weekly basis. In accordance with the preferences of my spouse, Susan, the desired value would amount to a null figure. She really hates them!

Although I do not frequently indulge, my spouse is amenable to my occasional enjoyment of cigars.

Regrettably, Tom stated that smoking is not permitted at the central fire pit. Nevertheless, there is another designated area along the pathway that caters specifically to individuals who engage in smoking. Shall we partake in refreshments and proceed towards that location?

I'm buying, Ryan insisted. What would you like?

Given that we have developed a more comprehensive understanding of one another, I shall proceed to request the production of my own unique mixture. It is a derivative of the Rob Roy cocktail. A refined blend of Scotch whisky, infused delicately with two premium maraschino cherries and a subtle infusion of cherry juice. The cherry juice exhibits a lighter quality than the sweet vermouth, with a more pronounced presence of the scotch flavor. I have added a touch of sweetness.

Ryan placed an order for Tom's beverage and procured for himself a straight pour of Jack Daniels. They obtained their beverages and proceeded towards the designated area for smokers' where a fire pit had been arranged.

No one was present when the men approached. They selected neighboring seats and arranged themselves for the purpose of facilitating conversation. Tom carefully positioned his beverage on the table adjacent to his seat, subsequently extracting the cigars from his pocket. The plastic wrappers emitted a gentle rustle as he deftly removed them from both cigars, presenting one to Ryan. I trust that you will find these to your liking. I have experimented with different brands, and upon recommendation from a friend, I have opted for these Rocky Patel LB1s. I have a deep affection for them, however, I am cognizant of the fact that individuals possess varying preferences.

Tom extracted a cigar lighter and cutter combination from his alternate pocket. Ryan, please utilize this tool for cutting and igniting the object.

Within a brief span of time, the cigars were ignited. The scent of premium cigar smoke permeated the surroundings.

Tom adjusted his position more comfortably in the chair. I am unable to comprehend the reasoning behind my spouse's aversion to the scent of cigars. In my opinion, the fragrance contributes significantly to the overall sense of tranquility that accompanies the experience.

Cheryl likes the smell. Ryan chuckled, expressing that had she been aware, she conceivably would have joined us.

Ryan, could you please elaborate on the characteristics that contribute to the quality of a cigar?

I don't know . . . Gentle flavor profile and a seamlessly consistent combustion.

Individual preferences may vary, however, a unanimous consensus can be reached regarding a harmonious combustion experience. One of the main factors contributing to my appreciation for Rocky Patel is their unwavering consistency. I can consistently depend on obtaining a uniform flavor profile in each and every cigar. Additionally, the Patels exhibit a consistent propensity for easy ignition, even combustion, and infrequent extinguishment. I am provided with a smooth draw that effortlessly enhances my experience, creating a sense of relaxation. And I do not believe it is a matter of chance.

One

Establishing the Qualities that Constitute an Effective Leader

The significance of an effective leader is indisputable. A leader assists individuals in their vicinity in surmounting obstacles and impediments. Executives possess the capability to enhance performance through:

Creating a Positive Vision

Effective leaders have the ability to unite their teams by establishing clear expectations regarding a positive outcome. It is equivalent to displaying postcards of that desired vacation destination you have always aspired to explore. The visuals serve as a source of inspiration and serve as a constant reminder to persistently pursue your aspirations in order to transform your dream journey into a tangible reality.

Leadership entails the skill of elucidating a vivid image to individuals, thereby enabling them to comprehend the rationale underlying their diligent endeavors. Leaders emphasize the potential outcomes that can be attained when the team perseveres in accomplishing the tasks at hand.

However, this is not accomplished solely by conjuring a vision without substance. Effective leaders conduct a thorough assessment of the team's capabilities in order to establish an attainable objective. Through conducting meticulous analyses of their team composition and the intricate circumstances they are likely to encounter, leaders possess the capability to formulate a vision that resonates with and elicits a comprehensive understanding from team members.

Leaders communicate their vision by weaving together captivating narratives and employing persuasive affirmations that facilitate collective recognition of achievable goals.

Inspiring others to Persevere

Possessing a vision is merely the commencement, and adept leaders comprehend this notion. They are aware that even the most carefully constructed plans can encounter setbacks. Projects often present difficulties that can appear insurmountable at times. Although a favorable perspective has the potential to generate enthusiasm among the team, leaders possess the ability to uphold this fervor by providing ongoing motivation.

Competent leaders possess the capability to inspire individuals during challenging circumstances. They dedicate time to acquire knowledge and comprehension of the individuals in their vicinity in order to effectively tackle any potential concerns that may arise. They employ a range of effective tactics to maintain consistent performance among their teams.

The strategies include:

Establishing appropriate expectations – Individuals who exhibit strong leadership abilities garner the trust of their teams by practicing transparency. They comprehend the significance of disclosing pertinent information (such as project expectations) as vital. When team members possess a comprehensive understanding of the forthcoming activities, it mitigates the prospect of encountering unforeseen and undesirable circumstances. As a result, individuals often exhibit a tendency to invest greater faith in their leaders.

Reiterating the vision - Excessive working hours and tight deadlines can lead individuals to lose sight of the initial vision that had aroused their enthusiasm for the project. Individuals expend a significant amount of energy initially, which can result in fatigue and eventual exhaustion within a few days. Leaders acknowledge the possibility of this occurrence and ensure the restatement of objectives in order to sustain the momentum.

Employing motivational measures – Though charm and charisma hold significance, effective leaders acknowledge the value of offering incentives to ignite motivation within their teams. These could take the form of financial incentives or exclusive rewards tailored to meet the preferences of their respective teams. As an illustration, gift certificates may be bestowed upon customer service representatives as a reward for consistently achieving elevated levels of customer satisfaction.

Devote yourself to assisting your colleagues.

Consistently summon the fortitude to express your thoughts and the determination to elucidate any uncertainties. Due to the burdensome weight carried by silences. And stones become walls. Ultimately, walls serve to create division.

Strive towards the contentment of your employees; in the event that they are not experiencing full satisfaction, endeavor to comprehend the underlying causes and, when feasible, endeavor to fulfill their requirements. An employee who displays high levels of motivation will significantly contribute to the company's success.

Customers are never prioritized!

Employees come first.

If you prioritize the well-being of your employees,

They will attend to the needs of your customers.

What assistance may I provide to you?"

An inquiry frequently posed by employees to their managers. Alternatively, a shift in mindset is imperative, whereby a prosperous manager manifests a willingness to serve their subordinates and provide aid during challenging circumstances, affording them comprehensive autonomy.

It is imperative for all individuals to receive adequate training and possess the necessary knowledge to fulfill their job responsibilities. In situations involving delicate matters, it is crucial for the manager to provide accessibility and assistance to their staff, thus facilitating the resolution of such issues.

Avoid constantly appearing overwhelmed or stressed; instead, display a willingness to assist and show understanding by positioning yourself as a resource for your employees.

A mere dedication of a few minutes each week to genuinely expressing interest in their endeavors can have a noticeable impact.

Do not engage in this task out of obligation, but rather out of a genuine desire to contribute to their welfare.

Demonstrate empathy effortlessly. It is an inherent trait possessed by certain individuals, while others may possess it to a lesser extent. However, it is imperative to bear in mind that disregarding this element is not permissible if one aspires to emerge as a triumphant leader.

Do not allow oneself to be engulfed by emotional upheaval, avoid moodiness, and instead strive to uphold self-composure that enables the impartial and clear evaluation of all encountered situations.

Frequently inquire with open-ended queries and attentively heed the responses provided. Demonstrate to your employees an authentic concern for their perspectives and the value of their contributions.

Occasionally, endeavor to subtly communicate to them that you are available to assist or lend support in the event they require aid or wish to apprise you of their personal circumstances or aspirations. Rest assured, your willingness to provide assistance remains unwavering.

Certainly, individuals should not necessarily perceive a sense of obligation, yet it is important to acknowledge that personal matters can indeed influence one's ability to effectively fulfill job responsibilities. Establishing a level of trust and open communication with one's manager can prove beneficial in allowing them to gain insight into one's emotional wellbeing at any given time.

As an illustration, it serves no purpose to exert excessive strain or coerce an employee who is undergoing the process of divorcing his spouse. It would be advisable to grant him a brief respite or refrain from allocating an excessive workload or stringent time constraints to him in the interim.

To adequately comprehend this mindset, it is imperative for a connection to exist where the employee feels comfortable enough to disclose personal thoughts and feelings to their supervisor. And establishing such a rapport necessitates a significant investment of time.

Utilize business trips, corporate events, or official dinners as opportunities to enhance your understanding of your employees. It is in these informal settings, beyond the confines of the workplace, where you can genuinely grasp the perspectives, emotions, concerns, and desires of the individuals with whom you collaborate on a daily basis.

It is imperative to prioritize the physical and mental wellness of employees, regarding them as individuals, consistently acknowledging and appreciating their contributions.

Simultaneously, endeavor to uphold an appropriate level of proximity. They ought to perceive you as an ally, rather than a companion, an individual who resides among them while remaining distinct from their group. It is imperative to establish this distinction of roles, as failure to do so may lead to confusion among your team members.

Prioritize your employees, demonstrating your commitment to invest in their professional development, thereby fostering a positive work environment.

Consistently provide them with encouragement and in the event that an error is made, ensure that the mistake is recognized and acknowledged. It is a display of conduct that will not be perceived as a sign of vulnerability, but rather recognized and contribute to earning respect and admiration.

How To Demonstrate Professionalism And Foster Positive Relationships With An UnfavorableCoworker To Effectively Advance In The Workplace

If one maintains utmost honesty, there will inevitably come a time when they find themselves in the presence of a colleague whom they find insufferable.

Merely catching sight of her graceful stride as she approaches your office can trigger a visceral discomfort in the depths of your stomach. The mere presence of her incites a heightened level of preparedness, akin to reaching Defcon 4.

However, given the necessity of collaborating, you gracefully maintain a pleasant facade, concealing any personal grievances.

Your Smile is Lying

Here\\\'s the problem.

Are you aware that one's genuine emotions invariably manifest in their vocal tone?

Regardless of how one attempts to conceal it, anger will inevitably become evident. In the event that you are feeling apprehensive, any semblance of a tremor or uncertainty will be evident in your vocal delivery. If you are not engaged, it will detract from the inherent harmony typically present when you are in a positive state.

May I inquire as to what the proposed solution might be?

Acting classes?

No.

Would terminating the individual be a viable course of action in light of the irreconcilable differences?

That could possibly be considered permissible within a legal context when dealing with divorce proceedings, yet it would not be deemed appropriate within a professional setting.

Surely that could not possibly be the predominant factor, correct?

Given the gravity of the situation, please continue perusing the following information.

It is a fact that not everyone will be to your liking. Not everyone can be your closest confidant. When Will Rogers made the statement that he had not encountered anyone with whom he did not find favor, he was being untruthful.

The key lies in confronting that actuality and positioning yourself strategically to accomplish your tasks.

The Power of Forgetting

We make concerted efforts to accurately retain all information, don't we?

When one fails to recall someone's name, they experience a sense of remorse upon encountering that individual subsequently.

When an individual gives their word, they experience a sense of remorse when the person to whom the promise was made happens to remind them, only to discover that the commitment had completely escaped their memory.

Upon arriving home, you discover that you inadvertently neglected to make the necessary stop to purchase milk, as you initially intended, when you proceed to open the refrigerator to retrieve some.

It is a common occurrence among individuals of the highest caliber.

However, there are instances when it can be highly beneficial to let go of certain things.

The most advisable course of action when faced with the challenge of collaborating with a person who entirely irritates you is to consciously set aside your feelings of disdain.

I surmise you might be contemplating, "Indeed, it is highly improbable for me to accomplish such a task."

If you are unable to do so, then you will be in a state of complete stagnation.

Three Justifications for Overlooking Your Displeasure Towards That Irritating Colleague

Below are a few key points to bear in mind when encountering an individual who poses challenges in your life.

5 – Enhancing Your Reputation through Efforts

A leader who possesses an esteemed and formidable reputation holds the potential to exert influence over others from the very outset. If one gains popularity as a leader, their reputation will precede them to their prospective followers. Individuals will eagerly anticipate collaborating with you. They will desire to become your apprentice as you hold a notable position within your industry.

In order to cultivate such a reputation, it is necessary to strategically shape one's image and commence accumulating notable accomplishments.

Ensure the contentment of your superiors.

It is imperative to maintain the satisfaction of your superiors and uphold strong affiliations with them. A considerable proportion of individuals tend to depart from their current employment having fostered strained relationships with their former superiors. This action typically has negative consequences with respect to one's professional trajectory.

When occupying a role within a professional setting, it is advisable to prioritize the satisfaction of those in authority. When concluding your tenure with the organization, it is prudent to maintain a harmonious rapport with your supervisor, allowing for the possibility of seeking their endorsement for future endeavors. It is equally advantageous for the advancement of your professional trajectory to abstain from engaging in any conflicts with them, as you may yet rely on their support in future endeavors.

Likewise, endeavor to exhibit mindfulness towards the sentiments of your superiors. Similar to individuals in general, bosses possess a propensity towards being preoccupied with safeguarding their reputations. Despite having completed all the tasks associated with a given project, it remains imperative to duly recognize the involvement and contributions of your superiors throughout the entirety of the undertaking. Make an effort to acknowledge their contributions by recognizing the value of their advice and the quality of their decision-making throughout the entire process.

If you appropriate full credit from your superiors, it may inadvertently elicit feelings of wounded pride, potentially jeopardizing your professional standing. Failure to acknowledge their contributions in the slightest may incite feelings of envy towards your accomplishments. A few individuals might experience a sense of insecurity and interpret your actions as attempts to encroach upon their professional roles.

You should aim to avoid cultivating such a relationship with your superiors. You aim to maintain their contentment until such time that you are prepared to find a suitable replacement.

Conceal your personal objectives from both superiors and subordinates.

Similar to the aforementioned company or organization, you possess an individual aspiration that you seek to accomplish. It would be advisable to maintain confidentiality regarding these personal goals, both in the presence of your superiors and subordinates. When individuals gain insight into your objectives, they are more likely to exploit your vulnerabilities. They will readily correlate your conduct with your underlying intentions. The more astute individuals within your organization will possess the ability to anticipate your future actions, as they possess an acute understanding of your desires.

By maintaining an aura of secrecy regarding your intentions in the presence of others, you can enhance the element of unpredictability in your actions. Suppose your aspiration is to acquire the position of Chief Executive Officer within your organization in the future. The incumbent CEO may perceive your intentions as implying a desire to assume his position. Additional individuals who are striving for the position may engage in actions that undermine your prospects in order to minimize the level of competition for the coveted spot.

By maintaining secrecy regarding your intentions, you can effectively strategize and work towards your objective without encountering hindrances from others. You allow interested individuals to contend for the position while amassing resources to advance your personal campaign.

One can maintain an air of secrecy regarding their intentions within the organizational context by refraining from divulging excessive information. If aspiring to assume the role of company president, it is advisable to exercise discretion in refraining from discussing such ambitions with individuals within one's immediate social circle.

If you intend to resign from your current employment in order to establish your own enterprise in the future, it is advisable to refrain from disclosing your intentions until you are prepared to disassociate yourself from the organization. The information has the potential to be communicated to your higher-ranking authorities who could potentially adopt measures to impede your progress, endeavors, or achievements, as a means to discourage your departure from the organization.

Exercise caution in the preservation of your intentions within your consciousness. During casual conversations, it is not uncommon for individuals to inquire about your personal aspirations. Ensure you have a prepared script to confidently address this inquiry. In general, it might be more expedient to conform your responses to their desires in order to deter further interrogations.

In order to maintain confidentiality, it is advisable to exercise restraint in your responses when discussing your desired outcomes. When engaging in conversation with your employer, it is advisable to exercise restraint in your responses, particularly when the topic of promotion is being discussed, especially if you are not yet prepared to actively pursue such opportunities. Rather, you should demonstrate interest in it only when you have the opportunity to acquire it.

Should you prematurely reveal your interests, individuals with ulterior motives may employ this information to manipulate and influence your conduct. Both your superiors and subordinates will attempt to accomplish this. In the course of this endeavor, you will be prioritizing their desires over your individual aspirations.

What is the theory of the box?

It is widely acknowledged that self-deception refers to the tendency to behave in a manner that contradicts one's personal beliefs and principles, yet individuals subsequently strive to reassure themselves that their actions are justified. In light of the fact that individuals unknowingly foster cognitive patterns and reactions to various challenges and circumstances, they eventually formulate convictions that attribute their actions to external forces such as people and events. To put it differently, we deceive ourselves while attributing responsibility to others for our own actions.

When one finds themselves caught in a recurring pattern of acting in opposition to their deeply-held principles, they have effectively confined themselves within the confines of a restrictive framework. Once you have confined yourself within the confines of a limited perspective, your perception and interaction with others become increasingly influenced by the veil of self-delusion. One ultimately loses perspective on others and subsequently engages in fault-finding and blaming, as a means to validate oneself. The individual ceases to embody their personhood and instead manifests as an impediment, an annoyance, or a predicament. As you shift accountability onto others, the individual you are attributing fault to will reciprocate by assigning blame to you. This implies that by residing within the confines of the box, you are effectively endorsing and fostering an environment within which your fellow team members also adhere to the same restricted mindset. This ultimately leads to a state where one becomes excessively focused on oneself rather than prioritizing the attainment of desired outcomes. The implication of this statement is that your current priority has shifted towards the final outcome of the project, rather than concentrating on accomplishing the intended objectives.

The phenomenon of self-deception can manifest in various ways. Presented herewith is a concise inventory delineating select behavioral patterns characteristic of individuals exhibiting a proclivity towards self-deception.

Overstating the deficiencies of others;

Boasting about your own merits;

Exaggerate the significance of the factors that support your self-delusion;

Attributing your own failures to external factors.

Presented below are two illustrations, one portraying an individual enclosed within the box, while the other depicts an individual situated outside the box.

Illustration One: An individual of the female gender occupies a seat on a public transportation vehicle, while simultaneously storing a receptacle containing purchases in close proximity. She is engaging in a digital entertainment activity on her mobile device. The bus decelerates, prompting the woman seated within to cast a brief upward glance and observe a considerable crowd poised to embark onto the bus. Instead of helping someone else by creating a seat out of her shopping bag, she chooses to feign intense concentration on her phone, oblivious to the individuals who remain standing throughout the entire duration of her bus journey. The lady is currently located inside the box. She perceives the presence of an individual seated beside her on the bus as a potential source of apprehension, devoid of regarding the remaining passengers as individuals possessing emotions and requirements.

Alternative phrasing: "Illustration Two: An individual of the female gender is seated in a bus that has reached its maximum capacity, and upon the arrival of additional passengers, she becomes aware of a mother accompanied by her offspring boarding the vehicle." The mother instructs her child to occupy the vacant seat adjacent to the lady, positioning herself alongside the child owing to the fact that the singular remaining unoccupied seat is situated at the opposite extremity of the bus. The lady who initially boarded the bus graciously offers her seat to the mother and relocates to the rear of the bus, facilitating the mother and child to be seated together. The woman is absent within the confines of the box. She demonstrates an understanding of the fellow passengers' intrinsic humanity and acknowledges their needs and emotions. Going beyond her own self-interest, she actively took measures to address both the mother and child's requirements, rather than simply retaining her seat and assuming that someone else would assist them.

Fostering Loyalty

Loyalty is reciprocal in nature; it entails equal responsibility for both the leader and the follower. It is of utmost importance to cultivate a sense of loyalty among the individuals under our leadership. If individuals lack a sense of allegiance towards you, and are propelled by diverging motives, they will promptly abandon their commitments when presented with an alternative. If individuals are solely motivated by financial gains in their employment with you, they are likely to swiftly seek opportunities elsewhere as soon as better monetary prospects arise. You aim to cultivate more profound emotional connections with your teams.

What is Loyalty?

Initial efforts should be directed towards obtaining a comprehensive understanding of the concept of loyalty. Initially, one might perceive the inclusion of this segment as trivial, as the concept of loyalty is widely understood by all. However, when seeking the perspective of two distinct individuals regarding the concept of loyalty, one will inevitably encounter two disparate interpretations.

During my time in secondary education, I came across an enlightening article within a periodical that delved into the concepts of camaraderie and steadfastness. According to the aforementioned article, the most effective method of assessing an individual's amicability and devotion entails embarking on a journey by car to ascertain if they remain alert or succumb to slumber. The individual who falls asleep during your driving is displaying a lack of loyalty. I initially found it preposterous, but my conviction shifted upon conducting this experiment which resulted in the adjacent individual succumbing to slumber. Upon careful consideration and subsequent examination, it became evident to me that the aforementioned test was erroneous in its assessment, leading me to initially believe that this individual possessed a genuine sense of loyalty. However, several months later, I was deeply betrayed by this person, and further investigation revealed a recurring pattern of such behavior on their part. It has been determined that the test is indeed efficacious.

Another matter regarding loyalty arises: in the event of an assault on my person, would you be inclined to intervene on my behalf? Would you be willing to provide protection and support for me in the face of both emotional and physical harm? I previously possessed an acquaintance whose companion fellvictim to an altercation perpetrated by a group of individuals during the nocturnal hours, subsequent to their departure from a local eatery in England. Subsequently, my acquaintance intervened, assuming a role of advocate for the individual, yet the latter swiftly departed the scene, leaving him abandoned in his efforts. In the ultimate consequence of a treacherous companion, my acquaintance suffered the permanent loss of their ocular organ.

Despite enduring the loss of his eye, he maintained his friendship with the individual who manifested cowardice during their shared experience. Subsequently, that very acquaintance caused significant damage to his business a couple of years following. My acquaintance possessed an extraordinarily well-received website alongside an exceptional online discussion platform, replete with highly commendable individuals engaging in noteworthy dialogues – to which even I contributed as a participant. This individual modified all of the passwords and proceeded to erase all data. He exhibited tremendous disloyalty, leading to severe consequences such as the permanent loss of a friend's vision, the usurpation of his business, and its subsequent ruination.

It is imperative to establish a clear definition when contemplating the concept of loyalty. We readily observe certain shared attributes and qualities:

an indication of dedication or the display of such dedication

a perception that individuals are mutually aligned or engaged in a reciprocal exchange a readiness to commit oneself to supporting the other individual in attaining their objectives

a sense of reverence - it is impossible to demonstrate loyalty towards an individual whom one does not hold in high regard

Above all, it is crucial to establish your own understanding and interpretation of loyalty. Does your understanding of loyalty encompass individuals who choose to remain at the office beyond their designated working hours, offering assistance in completing a project, despite not receiving overtime compensation? Does your interpretation of loyalty entail the scenario where the employer willingly decreases their own salary in order to compensate the employees for their additional hours worked?

I kindly request that you allocate a portion of your time for contemplation regarding your personal interpretation of loyalty, and subsequently integrate it into our forthcoming discussions. When engaging in conversations, I promptly communicate my interpretations and definitions of loyalty. In the course of one's life, as well as in the lives of the majority of individuals, the presence of loyalty circles can be observed. My primary allegiance lies with my wife and children, followed by my extended family, and finally, my staff. In addition to those individuals, there exist my readers and followers. I do not possess a greater level of loyalty towards you compared to my wife. I understand that you do not anticipate such a disparity, and I do not anticipate parity in return from you.

Loyalty is contingent upon the intrinsic characteristics of our interpersonal connections. The loyalty exhibited in a friendship differs from the loyalty expected in a professional relationship between a boss and an employee. Several years ago, I erred by attempting to manage my business in a manner akin to a personal friendship, extending familial treatment to all individuals involved. I expressed, "Rest assured, your employment is secure, and you have a permanent position in my team," resulting in a notable decline in their productivity. I employed individuals who were compensated with substantial sums, despite the fact that their actual work tasks carried a significantly lower value. I employed individuals whose weekly work commitment typically extended to less than one hour. Attempting to establish a familial unit in an unsuitable setting necessitated the dismissal of all personnel and recommencement of the process. I currently maintain exclusively professional relationships with my team members, resulting in heightened effectiveness. We are aligned with our business objectives. My attempt to integrate my business objectives with my family aspirations proved unsuccessful.

Three: Acquainting Oneself with Leadership Styles

In order to gain a profound comprehension of servant leadership, it is imperative to possess an understanding of the various forms of leadership. The leader must engage in self-evaluation to discern and acknowledge the inherent leadership style they possess. This will facilitate a more discerning assessment to effectively steer the team. Individuals have the ability to perceive when a leader is insincere in presenting oneself. Exhibit genuineness and unwavering consistency in your leadership of the team. Employing an artificial manner will engender an air of ambiguity and cast doubt upon your capacity to assume a leadership role. Every leadership style possesses its individuality, and depending on the circumstances at hand, you will employ one style in preference to another. The bedrock of leadership will provide you with direction regarding the optimal approach to adopt. There exists no mystical formula for achieving success. Each scenario is carefully assessed in order to determine the optimal course of action. In the year 1930, Lewin established three distinct leadership styles rooted in psychology: autocratic, democratic, and laissez-faire. To this day, these styles continue to be extensively employed as descriptors of leadership styles.

Autocratic Style

The autocratic approach requires immediate adherence. As the term suggests, this is the type of leader who strictly adheres to instructions and directives. This type of leadership approach is recommended in circumstances that necessitate prompt and decisive action. Nevertheless, if used in a continuous manner, it is likely to generate discontentment among the team. This particular approach proves to be efficacious in evacuating individuals from a building engulfed in flames or from an area exposed to gunfire. It demonstrates efficacy in situations involving a code or within the critical care unit, specifically for individuals experiencing cardiac arrest. Modifying the behavior of our team is typically unproductive and frequently encountered with opposition. Exercise prudence while utilizing it.

Democratic Style

The democratic approach involves achieving consensus by means of active participation. The democratic leader is an individual who establishes trust and accomplishes objectives by means of the electoral process, achieving consensus, or fostering collaboration. This specific type of leader inclines towards inquiring and achieving consensus. Please take into account this approach when implementing a new process or initiative. Establish a small focal group to delineate the process, anticipations, workflow, and other related matters. There will consistently be aspects that elude your consideration due to your limited engagement in the day-to-day operations. Kindly request the presence of your subject matter experts (abbreviated as SMEs) and engage in collaborative efforts. This will additionally create an opportunity for the team's endorsement.

Laissez-Faire Style

The laissez-faire approach involves the ideology of fostering a cohesive team and adopting a hands-off approach. It stands in direct contrast to autocratic leadership. In this context, the individuals are presented with objectives and goals that are characterized by a relatively flexible definition. One of the foremost advantages resulting from this particular approach is the promotion of innovation. This particular style may prove vexing for individuals seeking explicit and well-defined objectives. In the year 1964, the individuals of Robert Blake and Jane Mouton directed their attention towards two distinct styles, namely task-oriented and people-oriented, with a primary emphasis on business matters.

Task-Oriented Style

An approach centered on achieving outcome-based results characterizes the task-oriented style. In this manner, the leader ensures effective communication and establishes precise expectations regarding the objectives and intended outcomes. The assessment of the most suitable person for the task is not taken into account.

People-Oriented Style

The people-centric approach revolves around assessing the aptitude, enthusiasm, and professional growth of individual team members to ascertain their optimal suitability for specific tasks. This approach proves to be highly effective in fostering personal growth through challenging opportunities. Stretch opportunities are assignments assigned to individuals that surpass their current skillset and are designed to challenge and motivate them to expand their capabilities and foster growth. In the year 2002, an elaborate exposition was presented by Daniel Goleman, delineating the six distinctive emotional styles of leadership characterized as visionary, coaching, affiliate, democratic, pacesetting, and commanding.

SOCIAL SKILL MANAGEMENT

The Importance of Social Skills in Everyday Life

E

Having exceptional interpersonal abilities enables you to consistently project your most favorable image to individuals in your vicinity. They possess the capability to instill in you the self-assurance requisite for triumph in every circumstance, as well as the competence to establish meaningful connections with individuals you aspire to develop close relationships with. By acquiring the ability to recognize your own strengths and effectively engage in conversations, your social skills will grant you the opportunity to cultivate more profound interpersonal relationships. Irrespective of the individual with whom you engage in conversation, the ability to interact, engage socially, and develop a comprehensive understanding of another's persona serves as a significant elevation of self-assurance. This interconnectedness is what instills a sense of personal safety and confidence in both oneself and one's interactions.

Although socialization is profound and integral, it can pose challenges for certain individuals. Summoning the bravery to engage in conversation with another individual can frequently prove daunting, particularly when one's self-assurance is not firmly established. Numerous individuals encounter difficulties in their interpersonal aptitudes, yearning to possess a greater proficiency in the abilities that effortlessly manifest in others. Through consistent application, the techniques outlined in this guide seek to empower individuals, imbuing them with a sense of ease and self-assurance when engaging in social interactions, irrespective of geographical or situational context. By engaging in the practice of improving your body language and acquiring effective communication skills, you will undoubtedly cultivate a revitalized sense of self-assurance.

Commencing from the inception, you shall gain insight into the proficiencies that you currently possess. Through the utilization of your inherent strengths, surmounting your weaknesses can be facilitated. Rather than experiencing a sense of shame with regards to your weaknesses, you will acquire the skills necessary to convert them into attributes that will facilitate smoother social interactions. If the presence of shyness poses as a hindrance in your life, you will acquire the knowledge and skills to effectively overcome it through strategies that enable you to maintain your personal comfort while also projecting a more extroverted demeanor. By enhancing your self-esteem and subsequently boosting your charisma, you will experience a heightened sense of confidence, enabling you to proficiently navigate any social engagements that may arise.

One of the most challenging aspects of socialization arises when one engages with unfamiliar individuals. Due to their recent introduction into your life, you typically lack any sense of ease or familiarity to depend upon. Through acquiring the skills to initiate conversations with assurance and identify shared interests with individuals, you will come to discern that establishing relationships with unfamiliar individuals is an attainable endeavor. Regardless of the initial challenges, the process of socialization inevitably becomes smoother with increasing experience.

The present interpersonal connections that you maintain in your life are equally indispensable. After establishing a rapport with an individual, it is imperative to sustain this relationship through conscientious efforts to engage in social interaction. This guide aims to instruct and equip you with a plethora of strategies and methods that can be effectively employed across diverse social settings, thereby enabling you to achieve the desired outcome. Once you have incorporated these newly established practices, you will possess the ability to engage in conversation with individuals from all walks of life, irrespective of location, thereby emancipating yourself from any apprehensions or concerns associated with social interactions. The abilities acquired will endure indefinitely, serving as a perpetual reminder of your potential to engage in successful social interactions.

How Can They Establish Connections With Others?

ON THE PLAYGROUND

A

A gathering of young children, consisting of preschoolers and kindergarteners, are seated on the ground adorned in their smart, dark blue uniforms, complemented by charming pigtails, amidst the grassy area and mulch. One individual possesses lustrous, golden tresses, while the other adorns her braids with an elegant crimson ribbon. They are incredibly endearing; their small voices have recently molded their vocabulary words, with the Ls still sounding like Ys and the words lacking precision. How beautifully and self-assuredly they communicate with one another. They are in the process of creating a garden and engaged in a conversation about the method of excavating with the given tool in order to achieve the desired depth for planting various vegetation. One individual among them rises with the intention of gathering a few petite leaves from the adjacent shrub in order to "cultivate in the garden."

Shortly thereafter, Angela, a girl of identical age, makes her way towards the scene She is currently seeking companions to engage in play with, and has been moving from one social circle to another in an attempt to ascertain with whom to spend her time today. I have been closely observing her. Her mother is a concerned individual who is a client of ours, seeking assistance regarding her daughter's social challenges. Therefore, I am present to attentively observe and gather information.

Angela expresses her desire to join their illustrious club dedicated to the art of gardening. She seizes a wooden implement and commences excavating in proximate vicinity to the other young females. What activities are all of you engaged in? I would also like to engage in play with you. Can I help?"

Due to her enthusiastic disposition, she remains oblivious to the fact that she has inadvertently encroached upon the neighboring girls' excavation, resulting in a disheveled state. The pleasant exchange amongst the quartet of young ladies undergoes an abrupt shift in demeanor.

We are currently exerting considerable effort towards this endeavor." "We are exclusively handling this task." Promptly, the elder girl establishes certain limitations, restricting the inclusion of any additional individuals into the group. I find it astonishing how swiftly the atmosphere has transitioned, from affectionate cooperation to an abrupt shift towards individual isolation.

Angela responds with a retort, questioning, "Why is it that you never desire to engage in activities with me?" "Why is it that you consistently display a lack of desire to establish a friendship with me?!" Her vocal tone escalates, reaching a piercing level, and it is evident that she is on the brink of experiencing an emotional outpouring.

I cautiously approach, hesitating to intervene and wishing to allow events to unfold naturally. Yet, simultaneously, I recognize her need for guidance on engaging with others, and their need for instruction on accepting a new companion. There appears to be a recurring pattern in the conversation where Angela consistently requests to participate in activities with others without knowing how, resulting in a consistent response from the others along the lines of "we have already commenced." Consequently, Angela rapidly adopts a confrontational demeanor.

Certainly, upon further observation, it becomes evident that Angela has consistently encountered the same situation in every social circle she has attempted to join. An issue has arisen where there is a hindrance in her ability to establish connections with others.

This scenario has unfolded repeatedly on the playground throughout the span of the eighteen years I have been associated with this educational institution. People of various age groups, while on break, grapple with the challenge of socializing with one another.

Where do they belong? Which group? How do they connect? What is the basis for their sense of worth? How do they find a friend? Upon whom can they rely to serve as their companions? Despite the presence of numerous peers in the playground, a significant number of children experiences a sense of solitude.

At present, upon anticipating Angela's impending emotional breakdown, I discreetly escort her to a private space and provide her with a set of instructions to initiate collaboration with her female counterparts. It works. She fosters encouragement among the others and employs a more delicate form of communication. She refrains from disrupting their current storylines and instead embarks on investigating, conversing, and engaging with them. Once more, the discussion shifts towards affectionate subjects regarding floral arrangements, the delicate elegance of daisies and butterflies, enchanting unicorns, and the anticipation of cultivating magnificent gardens. So, I leave.

Indeed, shortly thereafter I discern a renewed sense of agitation. Angela has begun instructing others on their actions. It is crucial to ensure that you place the flowers within that specific location, on the designated side, as opposed to the other side. I've previously mentioned to you the necessity of watering these plants, as failure to do so will result in the wilting of the flowers. What type of garden are you endeavoring to create, if I may inquire? "Why are you disregarding my words?" She has assumed an authoritative demeanor, causing a lack of willingness in others to adhere to her directives. She begins to perceive it as a personal matter. She rushes towards me, overcome by tears. I find it difficult to establish friendships with others. I hate it here. I desire to return to my place of residence. "I am devoid of affection." Tears are streaming down her face.

I vividly recall the oscillations and fluctuations. I recall expressing a desire to engage in recreational activities with my acquaintances, although lacking the appropriate skills or means to do so. I recollect my acquaintances declining my company due to my perceived authoritative nature. Do these conversations align with the nature of our past discourse?

Once more, I attentively listen and proceed to provide her with the appropriate expressions, collaborating with her and the other young ladies to analyze and organize the information. I am cognizant of the fact that I will have to repeat this process multiple times until they become at ease. Hence, we incorporate empathy courses within the morning spiritual classes.

Nevertheless, not all parents are privileged with the knowledge of effectively engaging with their children. Not all parents have the opportunity to observe their children interacting at the playground during snack and lunch breaks, analyzing areas of improvement, and assisting them in effective communication to express their needs and comprehend one another.

I am confident that you have been privy to numerous discussions of this nature with your child, and it is likely one of the motivations behind your decision to engage with this book. Multiple factors are at play in this situation. The primary consideration lies in the fact that the young child lacks the ability to establish connections with others.

There are no hidden formulas or clandestine methods to achieve success. It is the outcome derived from thorough preparation, diligent effort, and the acquisition of knowledge through trial and error.

- Colin Powel

In India, apart from urban regions, there is a limited prevalence of families who raise their daughters with a focus on cultivating a prosperous professional trajectory. Regrettably, the notion of pursuing a career is consistently viewed as discretionary for this particular group. The majority of young women are not afforded the opportunity to engage in casual social interactions with their neighbors or extended family members, thereby leading to the development of feelings of inferiority from an early age.

Education is a crucial absent characteristic in the majority of such instances. Until such time as this circumstance undergoes a transformation, the prevalence of crimes resulting from women's lack of awareness would persist. In urban areas, children are raised in an environment characterized by gender equality, instilling in them the value of pursuing a career that aligns with their aspirations. This has resulted in the equitable appreciation of both genders. It is essential for every parent to exercise great caution in instilling this powerful message from their earliest years of upbringing. This initiative has the potential to cultivate accomplished female leaders.

IndraNooyi, who previously held the position of Chief Executive Officer at PepsiCo, has consistently been listed as one of the top 100 most influential women globally by Forbes magazine. Presently, she holds a position on the board of directors for both Amazon and the International Cricket Council. Nooyi, hailing from Chennai, located in the state of Tamil Nadu, acquired her undergraduate education at Madras Christian College and pursued further studies at the esteemed Indian Institute of Management in Calcutta. Subsequently, she pursued her master's degree in Public and Private Management at Yale University in the United States.

In the initial phase, while she obtained financial assistance from Yale, she had to undertake the role of an overnight receptionist in order to meet her monetary requirements. She lacked the financial means to purchase a formal ensemble in order to effectively present herself during interviews at business consulting firms. However, she possessed a distinct vision and unwavering enthusiasm to accomplish her goals.

Noted for her exceptional levels of vigor and diligent approach, Indra possessed a rich repertoire of roles within esteemed organizations such as Johnson & Johnson, Boston Consulting Group, Motorola, and ABB prior to her tenure at PepsiCo, which commenced in 1994. She spearheaded the development and reorganization of PepsiCo's global strategy. Additionally, she spearheaded the procurement of Tropicana, Quaker Oats, and various other entities, resulting in a substantial increase in the company's net annual profit from $2.7 billion to $6.5 billion. In 2006, she assumed the position of Chief Executive Officer of PepsiCo, where she remained in service for a tenure of 12 years. Over the span of her twenty-four years at PepsiCo, she spearheaded the incorporation of a greater array of health-conscious offerings into the company's extensive repertoire of food and beverage options. Throughout her term, the company experienced a remarkable growth in sales, with an increase of 80%.

She was bestowed with the prestigious Padma Bhushan award by the President of India. She held the second position in the Forbes ranking of The 19 Most Influential Women in the corporate world. She possesses an array of honorary doctorate degrees from multiple esteemed universities.

During a magazine interview, she expressed, "I find myself awakening in the middle of the night, jotting down various iterations of PepsiCo strategies on a sheet of paper." Unquestionably, she exemplifies exceptional leadership as the CEO and serves as an inspiring figure for countless entrepreneurs.

6

You consistently cause the glass to break.

The date of September 11, 2011 marked the significant milestone of the tenth commemoration of the terrorist attacks that targeted the United States. My wife, Debbie, and I departed from our residence on a delightful and unclouded evening in order to retrieve our daughter from a religious event taking place in the vicinity of Fort Collins. We were within a distance of less than two miles from our residence when I received a notification regarding a significant hazardous materials occurrence taking place at the intersection connecting U.S. Highway 34 and Interstate 25. Subsequently, a series of text messages rapidly arrived on my mobile device, signifying the occurrence of a significant emergency. We were situated in the northwest vicinity of the interchange, proceeding in an eastern direction. From this vantage point, we had an unobstructed line of sight towards the location of the occurrence. At a distance, I observed a luminous orange radiance illuminating the nocturnal expanse. In spite of the absence of light, a substantial and obscure plume of smoke could be distinctly discerned emanating from the conflagration. Furthermore, I was also apprised of a text communication instructing off-duty personnel to promptly resume their duties.

The chief officers at Loveland Fire Rescue Authority are provided with a staff vehicle for the purpose of on-call duty and responding to off-duty emergencies as necessary. This was one of those circumstances in which it was imperative for me to provide a response.

As I veered towards the eastern direction on U.S. Highway 34, there was an unmistakable display of the incident's whereabouts, as the fiery spectacle stood prominently before me, casting its grandeur and brilliance. Upon arrival at the scene, I witnessed a horizontal gasoline tanker that was completely consumed by flames. Due to the fire's impact, the neighboring light pole exhibited signs of deformation and imminent collapse. I reported to the designated command center and was allocated the role of incident safety officer.

Prior to undertaking my responsibilities, the individual in charge of the operation apprised me of a distressing circumstance, revealing that the driver of the truck had been unable to emancipate himself and had succumbed to the mishap.

The truck was proceeding in a northerly direction along I-25 and proceeded to take an eastbound exit onto U.S. Highway 34. While executing a manoeuvre, the vehicle experienced a rollover, resulting in it tilting onto the driver's side of the truck cabin. Witnesses stated that the driver exhibited no signs of movement. Prior to anyone managing to reach him, a conflagration ensued, engulfing the aluminum container housing an estimated quantity of nine thousand gallons of gasoline. Considering the truck's placement and the unmistakable fatality, a collective determination was reached by Loveland Fire and the Colorado State Patrol to allow the fuel to combust. Ultimately, the chosen course of action proved to be more prudent, as it eradicated the need to manage sizable volumes of perilous, unignited gasoline and mitigated the risk of ecological harm.

Despite being at a considerable distance from the blazing inferno, the scorching heat emitted by the ferocious flames compelled me to lower my head in an effort to protect my face. Due to my eyes' sensitivity to light, I found myself narrowing my eyes in response to the intenseness of the flames. The conflagration also emitted a resounding, thunderous noise, coupled with enormous surges of ebony smoke intertwined with fiery hues of reddish-orange. Due to the incident, the closure of both I-25 and U.S. 34, prominent roadways in Northern Colorado, was implemented. The traffic congestion extended several miles due to the fascination it engendered among the inhabitants in the vicinity who were curious about the unfolding event. Regrettably, the driver's life was lost, but thankfully, no other individuals sustained injuries or fatalities. Over the course of my professional tenure, I have attended numerous fire incidents. That one will be etched into my memory for a long time.

Exhibiting empathy presents a formidable challenge for a servant leader to effectively acquire. As per the definition provided by Empathy Definition/What is Empathy (2009), empathy is an inherent emotional attribute that enables individuals to discern and understand the emotions of others, along with the ability to envision their thoughts and experiences. Humans, since the early stages of development, have possessed the capability to detect the emotional states of their caregivers and consequently express similar sentiments in their own unique manner. When our mothers experience discontentment, our own state of happiness is also affected, and conversely. Acknowledging that individuals possess unique viewpoints that differ significantly from our own necessitates the cultivation of empathy.

As per the findings of the researchers, there exist three distinct forms of empathy that facilitate individuals in perceiving the world through the lens of another individual's perspective. One of the initial components is the practice of perspective-taking, also known as cognitive empathy. Cognitive empathy refers to the capacity to envision oneself in the circumstances of another individual. This kind of empathy enables a leader to comprehend someone else's perspective without necessitating an emotional involvement, rendering it particularly advantageous for managers or servant leaders engaged in negotiations. Nevertheless, this approach has the disadvantage of restricting empathy as a result of cognitive empathy.

Emotional empathy can be considered as the most intrinsic form of empathy. Emotional empathy refers to the capacity to authentically share in the emotional experiences of another individual. One advantage of emotional empathy is its capacity to enable individuals to "vicariously perceive" the emotions of others. Consider individuals employed in compassionate professions such as healthcare, academia, or social services. The capacity to empathize with others' emotions enables a physician to appropriately and effectively respond to the needs of their patients. Additionally, it conveys the notion that individuals, particularly those in positions of authority, possess the capacity to react suitably when confronted with indications of sorrow or distress by their acquaintances, colleagues, and fellow community members. Notwithstanding, this form of empathy may occasionally be perceived unfavorably as excessively compassionate or even patronizing, especially when engaging with individuals belonging to diverse racial, ethnic, and socioeconomic backgrounds than that of the leader.

Finally, it is crucial to note that compassionate empathy encompasses the capacity to deeply comprehend and share in the emotional pain of another individual, thereby prompting one to undertake proactive measures to relieve their distress. Comprehensive understanding of others' emotions is frequently regarded as the most appropriate manifestation of empathy. The majority of individuals do not seek limited outcomes such as being comprehended cognitively (cognitive empathy) or receiving empathic consideration from others (emotional empathy). The majority of individuals aspire to obtain comprehension, compassion towards their circumstances, and, above all, a competent influencer who will proactively advocate for their interests or collaborate with them to rectify their issues. Achieving equilibrium poses a formidable task for a servant leader, as the display of emotional empathy can be misconstrued as excessive emotional involvement, while the manifestation of cognitive empathy runs the risk of being perceived as emotionally disengaged.

Detailed exploration of various facets of empathy can be found in Daniel Goldman's renowned publication from 2010, entitled 'Emotional Intelligence: Why It Can Matter More Than IQ.' Nonetheless, the servant leader, driven by their quest for a heightened sense of benevolence, endeavors to embody empathy as a means to grasp a profound understanding of others' needs and apprehensions, thereby enabling them to respond effectively. It is worth noting that a majority of individuals do exhibit empathy to a certain degree.

Goldman was the pioneering individual who initially emphasized the significance of comprehending others as an indispensable element of empathy. The servant leader demonstrates a conscientiousness in discerning and perceiving the emotional cues of others. This can be accomplished by engaging in active listening and being attentive to nonverbal cues. Leaders ought to demonstrate sensitivity and make an effort to comprehend alternative perspectives. Put differently, it is imperative for a leader to refrain from making judgments until they personally encounter the perspective of others or empathize by fully understanding their circumstances. Ultimately, a servant leader is equipped to better serve others by prioritizing their needs and emotions, as opposed to imposing their own beliefs without genuinely grasping the other individual's standpoint.

6.

INTELLECTUAL CURIOSITY

• • •

What is the significance of possessing a strong sense of intellectual inquisitiveness in the capacity of a recruiter? In a Fortune magazine interview on March 3, 2016, Jennifer Anderson, at the time serving as the Vice President of Talent Acquisition at Capital One, articulated that our organization identifies exemplary candidates through their profound intellectual inquisitiveness, genuine dedication to our mission and the pursuit of constructive transformation, as well as their inclination to cultivate leadership qualities with compassion and empathy.

This will delve into the definition and significance of intellectual curiosity, elucidate its cultivation methods, outline its assessment techniques, and underscore the advantages of employing intellectually inquisitive recruiters.

WHAT IS INTELLECTUAL CURIOSITY?

There exist various interpretations of the concept referred to as "intellectual curiosity," all of which encompass elements relevant to the sphere of recruitment to some extent or another. Intellectual inquisitiveness entails a desire for the acquisition of comprehensive knowledge, encompassing a wide range of subjects such as the composition of objects, underlying mechanisms, systems, mathematical correlations, languages, social norms, and history.

When discussing intellectual curiosity, it is crucial to consider the distinction between having a genuine pursuit of knowledge and being inquisitive about matters that do not contribute to the acquisition of comprehensive knowledge. We are keen on evaluating inquisitiveness that leads to acquisition of information pertinent to the recruitment process. Intellectual inquisitiveness engenders an active state of mind rather than a passive one, and individuals possessing this characteristic are those who yearn for personal growth. Inquisitive individuals consistently engage in pondering inquiries and seeking resolutions, thereby fortifying the power of their intellect. The development of our cognitive abilities can be likened to that of muscles, as the more we engage them, the greater their growth and intellectual development is influenced by the mental exercise of curiosity. The cultivation of intellectual curiosity is a vital factor in achieving success, as it can provide you with substantial support in your professional endeavors, on par with any other expertise. The impediment to inquisitiveness lies in one's self-awareness, which may stem from apprehensions about one's image, fear of posing unwise questions, or the unease of appearing inferior in the presence of the client. To be candid, it is probable that these concerns are originating from your own apprehensions. It is highly likely that adopting a more inquisitive stance during client interactions, and posing thought-provoking and informative questions, will not only better equip you for a fruitful search but also assist the client in gaining a more comprehensive understanding of the search objectives.

Four

Facilitating a Self-Exploration Inquiry: Discovering One's True Identity

Steve

Irrespective of whether the specific focus of their expertise lies in coaching leaders, each and every coach I am acquainted with eventually finds themselves involved in coaching individuals in leadership roles. Regrettably, numerous individuals find themselves daunted by this occurrence, as they hold the belief that high-ranking executives encounter unique and intricate challenges that can only be comprehended by coaches with direct experience in that particular sphere.

In the event that you find yourself in such a predicament, it is important to acknowledge the distinctions between coaching and consulting. Consulting entails a procedural approach that typically involves the provision of specialized advice by experts. On the other hand, coaching, at its optimal level of performance, enables the client to gain personal insights and explore new possibilities.

Numerous coaches who are engaging in their first experience of coaching leaders often commit the error of attempting, in an inelegant manner, to adopt a consulting role. They are inclined towards expeditiously addressing a particular issue. Occasionally, individuals endeavor to present themselves as more knowledgeable than their actual capabilities, despite the fact that the expertise they possess in understanding the intricate workings of the mind is precisely why the client seeks their assistance. They fail to grasp the profound impact that the client's acquired knowledge and subsequent personal growth through coaching can have, which often endures for an extended period.

When coaches prioritize the development of the individual player within the larger framework of the game, they have the greatest impact on a leader's professional growth.

When coaches bring attention and clarity to shifting a client's perceptions of failure, weakness, and "doing something wrong" into opportunities for increased curiosity and creativity, coaching value is highest.

Contemplating the emphasized transformation that Will Keiper has strongly advocated for leaders to undertake in order to achieve effectiveness and personal fulfillment, I posed the following question to myself: "In my capacity as a coach, what would be the most effective approach to assist a leader in making said transformation?"

My response involved analyzing each of Will's ten leadership principles and providing insights on how one could effectively guide a leader to adopt and implement them. Below are the responses I have provided, along with a range of techniques that all coaches may wish to contemplate implementing:

Fulfill your commitments as promised.

Many leaders fail to recognize the potency and influence wielded by their verbal expressions. They demonstrate a disregard for their commitments and show little concern for the consequences that ensue from their inability to fulfill their stated obligations. They possess a limited comprehension of the adverse impact that such behavior has on employee morale. It is difficult to effectively lead when individuals perceive the leader as lacking integrity.

The most effective approach to fostering integrity is to concentrate on harnessing its inherent positive influence. You desire for your leader-client to experience the enhanced vitality that arises from conscientiously upholding their commitments. You have the opportunity to enhance your client's comprehension regarding their adherence to their commitments, punctuality, and accountability.

It is truly enlightening and exhilarating when a leader (or any client) attains the ability to embody their commitments. This experience evokes a profound sense of empowerment, wherein one's words shape and manifest their reality.

Six common learning issues

Having examined several prevalent misconceptions regarding the process of learning and elucidated its nature, we shall now proceed to explore the predominant obstacles encountered by individuals in their pursuit of knowledge. While advancing through this section, consider the extent of each issue's pertinence to your specific circumstances.

Concern #1: There is an inclination towards excessive information acquisition

Many individuals attempt to acquire knowledge beyond their capacity for assimilation. They persist in engaging with literature, audio-visual materials, or auditory content, yet fail to allocate ample time for the comprehensive absorption of the subject matter they aim to acquire. Regrettably, the human brain is incapable of assimilating every single fragment of information that is presented to it.

When attempting to assimilate a surplus of information, we often encounter bewilderment rather than gaining additional knowledge. Our cognitive processes become disrupted, and we encounter difficulties in comprehending the extensive array of books, videos, podcasts, and articles that we have amassed throughout the years. Furthermore, it is highly likely that we retain only a minimal amount of the information we acquire.

I opine that there exist several rationales for our susceptibility to excessive learning, which encompass the following:

Lack of awareness. Frequently, we are unaware of the excessive amount of information that we are consuming. It transitions our cognitive faculties into a repository of superfluous fragments of information for which we lack a clear utility. Although we may possess recollections of factual information, statistics, or narratives, we encounter difficulties in effectively interconnecting them, leading us to overlook the overarching concept or main theme at hand.

Lack of clear goals. Without clearly defined objectives, we naturally become overwhelmed by an excessive amount of irrelevant information. Presently, it is not imperative for us to ingest every bit of information with a clear objective, however, it is more advantageous to establish a set of educational objectives to assist us in discerning and disregarding superfluous content.

Unquenchable thirst for knowledge. The pursuit of knowledge, if driven by a passion for learning, has the potential to evolve into an addictive tendency. Increasing our exposure to literature or engaging in a greater consumption of audio content creates a sense of acquiring knowledge, leading to a gratifying emotional experience. As an illustration, it can engender a feeling of superiority, as we acquire knowledge and exhibit higher intellectual capacities than our peers. Nevertheless, if we fail to allocate sufficient time for the purpose of reflecting on our studies, our retention abilities will be greatly limited.

What about you? Are you acquiring a significant amount of knowledge? It is acceptable if that is the case, as it signifies a steadfast commitment to acquiring knowledge. The essence lies in implementing a more efficient framework for your learning endeavors.

THE ROLE OF POLITICAL DIPLOMACY IN

CORPORATE AND APPLICATIONS

It has been repeatedly emphasized that we should exercise restraint in our discourse, speaking only when essential. There have been both literary and political tendencies to endorse the adverse ramifications of an "unreasonably vocal demeanor." The correlation between the business conglomerate has been repeatedly reaffirmed within business circles on numerous occasions. In this particular scenario, scholars and experts stress the importance of concealing the motives of the business organization, thereby acquiring a presumption of innocence (in relation to competing corporations), subsequently ascending discreetly. That assertion, while partly accurate, fails to take into account the comprehensive aspect of employing the strategy of concealing information by providing less than what is essential. Hence, we propose the adoption of an augmented principle of political discretion utilizing a strategy of veiled concealment, and the implementation of an amplified pursuit of objectives that are detached from the core purpose of the organization. What we intend to communicate is that remaining silent to mask corporate or individual goals is insufficient. We should strive to extend our efforts by refraining from diverting others' attention from our goals, not through silence, but by excessively discussing nonessential topics (in order to prevent any diversion from the focused pursuit of our objectives). The prevailing ideology regarding this matter of political diplomacy within the corporate realm posits that the deliberate creation of a diversionary trajectory (with the intention of redirecting competitive focus) engenders disorder in the cutthroat corporate environment, thereby enabling a particular corporate entity to introduce novel products or services into the market, thereby confounding other corporate organizations.

Psychological perspective: When we openly divulge our strategic plans in the public sphere, be it consciously or subconsciously, we unintentionally attract individuals within the corporate realm who become potential adversaries, hindering the successful implementation of our intended strategies. Hence, employing understatement as a means of concealment is a commendable psychological strategy, though an even more effective approach lies in the manifestation of enhanced diversionary tactics. Throughout history, humanity has displayed a strong inclination towards competitiveness. In both the realms of business and conflict, the significance of political diplomacy cannot be overstated. Several factors associated with diplomatic theory include: genetic behavior, cultural instincts in primates, and potential genetic variations. Through the implementation of diverse and intricate diversions within the business realm, we induce a subconscious state of relaxation in our competitors. Hence, it is imperative that we demonstrate this sophisticated political strategy within our corporate establishment and achieve substantial financial gains in our business endeavors.

BUSINESS INSIGHT: Through the utilization of a diversionary tactic (by abstaining from silence and instead amplifying irrelevant matters), we deceive competitor organizations. Furthermore, we experience growth through the means of deception.

Developing Your Team

Your team is your paramount asset. Their distinct aptitudes and principles will undoubtedly enhance collective achievements through seemingly arbitrary means. By means of personal and collective enhancement, one can gradually perceive the inherent patterns within the system, anticipate forthcoming occurrences, and adeptly employ appropriate methods of communication and management to effectively steer the situation towards the desired outcome.

Your team members possess significant value, and by dedicating time and effort to their development and fostering a collective perspective, you will not only witness personal growth as a leader but also unlock the full potential of your team. By effectively harnessing the individual skills of your team members in a strategic manner, you can enhance the overall efficiency of your entire process. As an exemplification, within a sales environment that relies on cold calling, one may discover the presence of a skilled individual designated as the "opener" who contacts clients and acquaints them with the company's offerings. Subsequently, the client is redirected to a proficient "closer" responsible for finalizing the sale.

Please refrain from becoming agitated or overly assertive, as this behavior is likely to provoke irritation among individuals on each occasion. You may indeed be correct, however, in accordance with Newton's principle of reciprocal action (wherein any action elicits an equal and opposite reaction), it is worth noting that pushing forward may be met with resistance from team members, superiors, as well as clients.

In order to effectively oversee the progress of your team on an individual and collective level, it is imperative to possess a comprehensive understanding of each team member's role, skills, and strengths, and determine the most optimal means of capitalizing on their abilities. Before commencing any collective endeavor, it is imperative for a leader to pose the subsequent inquiries to themselves:

Is it possible for us to successfully complete this task?

What resources are necessary to accomplish the task?

What existing resources do we possess?

What are our areas of expertise in this particular domain?

What are our weaknesses?

As an individual in a position of leadership, which specific leadership approach would be most effective in successfully accomplishing this task?

Please bear in mind: Cultivate, modify, and implement.

Keep in mind: In the role of a leader, your effectiveness is demonstrated by the seamless execution of tasks without drawing attention to your presence.

The Seven Stages

A team will typically traverse through a series of seven primary phases while working towards the accomplishment of a goal or collective undertaking. We could potentially attempt to expedite this process by omitting certain stages, however, those who choose to do so will inevitably learn from experience that any skipped stage will ultimately have to be revisited at a later time. Each of the seven stages presents its own set of challenges; these are effectively addressed by maintaining transparent communication and providing consistent feedback throughout the entire team. Every phase necessitates that a leader inquire certain inquiries to their team in order to assess progress. The responsibility to guide a team through the seven stages lies with the leader, who must initiate the process, thereby exposing themselves to the possibility of making mistakes. To prevent these errors from evolving into mistakes, it is imperative to promptly address them.

The initial phase of every undertaking is Orientation. At this juncture, a leader presents an overview of the prevailing circumstances, the pertinent course that brought us to this stage, the team's collective identity, as well as its fundamental purpose and values. The initial phase of orientation holds significant significance as it outlines the overarching trajectory and necessitated criteria for the team.

During the second phase, known as Conception or Brainstorming, the team is required to collectively exhibit the quality of being straightforward. A team that operates on a basis of reciprocal respect will contribute innumerable perspectives to the discussion. Should the brainstorming phase be neglected, the team's state may become one of uncertainty and disorientation, or, at worst, a state characterized by fear and lack of trust.

When delineating objectives and elucidating goals, the purpose is to precisely establish the requirements from each individual, their interconnected goals, and the collective vision embraced by the team in its entirety. Insufficient elucidation of individual roles and objectives within the team may incite skepticism regarding the overarching task, necessitating a subsequent revisit to this stage for a comprehensive explication.

The Commitment phase represents the ultimate stage in the culmination of the task's development. Presently, all individuals possess well-defined and quantifiable objectives, definitive choices have been determined, and the team is now fully prepared to take action. If not resolved, the commitment phase will have negative consequences, resulting in certain team members opposing the plan in its entirety. Others may acquiesce to the proposal, yet they will inevitably rely on others to execute the arduous tasks.

During the phase of Implementation, it is incumbent upon the leader to ensure that all individuals perform their designated tasks in a timely manner. This is accomplished by establishing explicit protocols that are in alignment with the abilities and principles of the team. Not adhering to this requirement will lead to the occurrence of deadlines being missed, conflicts arising, and confusion prevailing.

The Action stage is the phase in which all elements converge and synergize. If adequate attention has been devoted to the preceding phases, the implementation phase will proceed seamlessly and prove to be fruitful. The effective arrangement and harmonious collaboration of your team will give rise to extemporaneous outcomes, resulting in the consistent surpassing of your objectives. Exercise caution in ensuring that your team does not become overwhelmed, as this initial success may be overshadowed by future instances of burnout.

Conducting a post-mortem analysis is imperative in order to sustain our ongoing success. Acknowledging our triumphs and reflecting on the lessons we have garnered will impart us with endurance and inspiration for the subsequent undertaking. Debriefing serves to enhance our strategies through a meticulous analysis of our past actions, enabling us to identify the most effective approaches and areas for improvement. Adequate appreciation and commendation should be generously bestowed during this phase, as it will serve to divert feelings of monotony and exhaustion.

The seven stages occur organically, and through our acknowledgement and investigation of them, we can effectively utilize these stages as indicators of our advancement. Having a comprehensive understanding of the seven stages enables us to identify the origins of problems and address them in an efficient manner. It is imperative to accord due reverence to the seven stages, for they are not to be evaded.

In the event that your team is facing challenges, it is imperative to begin by referring to the seven stages and determining the precise stage your team is presently experiencing. Subsequently, it is essential to acknowledge and review the course of actions taken thus far until the root cause is uncovered. As previously indicated, an underlying issue will have minimal correlation to any specific individual, but rather pertain to the collective as a whole.

The Leadership Of Innovation

Amidst the intensifying global competition within the contemporary marketplace, the task of effectively competing and securing a profitable market share has become progressively challenging. Due to advancements in technology, the international business landscape has been significantly reduced, enabling organizations of all sizes and geographical locations to effectively engage and emerge victorious in the global marketplace. As a result of this phenomenon, certain companies have witnessed a transition where their offerings have become commoditized. In a business characterized by commodification, the pricing factor takes precedence as the primary determinant for customers in their contemplation of procuring your product or service. In the absence of a distinct and unparalleled competitive edge, these enterprises are compelled to rely exclusively on price-based competition, leading to minimal customer loyalty towards their respective establishments. This gives rise to a distinctive reliance on the prevailing economic and competitive forces that result in the closure of numerous companies.

In order to thrive in such a competitive landscape, it is imperative for organizations to establish a distinct competitive edge, enabling them to reduce their reliance on the economy or their rivals for success and sustainability. In order to flourish within such a dynamic milieu, it necessitates a distinctive breed of leader who possesses the acumen to foster a climate wherein their enterprise can establish and perpetuate their competitive edge amidst the expansive global market.

Solution

In order for an organization to discern its exclusive competitive edge, it is essential for the leader to guarantee that the organization is imbued with a sense of empowerment and receives ample support to establish a resilient competitive advantage that can be effectively cultivated and implemented. This poses several challenges for leaders/managers in contemporary organizations, as the typical member of the organization experiences apprehension about preserving their employment in order to safeguard their means of sustenance.

Presently, you are requesting the members of this organization to engage in a process of challenging the established methods of conducting business and potentially even altering the framework established by their leader/manager at the inception of the organization. This places a significant burden on the individuals within that organization. Particularly in a smaller organization, where individuals possess a familiarity with the individuals who initially implemented these specific products/processes, they are now being called upon to adopt a discerning perspective towards these identical products/processes. The leader/manager is now tasked with establishing a conducive environment wherein members are able to engage in the exploration of various strategies to cultivate a distinct competitive advantage for the organization while ensuring their safety and comfort.

What will be covered?

This book will encompass eight distinct dimensions pertaining to effective leadership. Allow us to provide you with a concise overview of the content encompassed in each chapter:

Prioritize Personal Development: Dedicate yourself to personal growth as the initial stride towards becoming an exemplary leader. There are no alternatives available. Within this chapter, we shall delve into the topic of cultivating personal growth as a leader, focusing on the development process from within. We will delve into the methods for developing the mentality of an exceptional leader. Furthermore, we will delve into the most effective leadership style that aligns with your preferences.

Goal Setting as Exemplified by a Leader: The establishment of goals constitutes merely one facet of achieving success. Additionally, the attainment of these objectives will be integral to the procedure. In the following section, we will explore the process of establishing objectives that can be readily accomplished by both yourself and your team on a consistent basis. Certainly, there will be challenges that need to be surmounted. Nevertheless, this process will render the establishment of objectives uncomplicated and unambiguous.

The essential elements for achieving success: strategic planning and meticulous organization are imperative for each leader in order to effectively manage their primary responsibilities.

What comes first? What responsibilities will be undertaken by the remaining members of your team? We shall delve into an examination of the process of planning and organizing, and further explore the imperative for leaders such as yourself to undertake corresponding actions.

Creating Results: Efficient Implementation: One aspect lies in the art of strategizing. However, the implementation process presents a contrasting narrative. No progress will be made if no action is taken. This aims to instruct you in the art of performing actions with utmost precision and decisiveness, surpassing any trace of hesitancy.

One's strength is determined by the weakest member: We will discuss the typical strengths and weaknesses that leaders confront frequently. If an individual possesses shortcomings, this shall impart knowledge on how to ameliorate said weaknesses, ultimately transforming them into inherent strengths.

Enabling the Growth of Your Team: It is imperative for a leader to instill motivation, inspiration, and empowerment within their team. This disparity can be indicative of a company characterized by robust morale and productivity as opposed to one marked by a lackluster and apathetic atmosphere.

Performance Management: This will aid you in assessing the performance of your team. Which individuals are actively engaged in their work and making meaningful contributions, and which individuals are not? Within this guide, you will encounter various strategies that can facilitate your ability to motivate team members who require improvement or are at risk of sanctions.

Leadership requires continuous commitment: Your duties as a leader extend beyond that. Whether you find yourself in a professional or domestic setting, it is incumbent upon you to demonstrate and utilize your leadership skills. We will discuss its potential applications beyond the professional realm.

It is the appropriate time to enact a daring action.

The subsequent challenge has the potential to be a considerably arduous endeavor. You are presented with two alternatives:

You have the option to keep this book in storage and refrain from further reading. And your abilities to lead will remain consistent. Lack of effective communication, absence of decisive decision-making, and inability to galvanize one's team.

OR

Persist in advancing your leadership abilities and fostering personal growth, enabling you to confidently confront and overcome challenges. Establish objectives, strategize and organize, grant authority to your team, and ensure their steadfast commitment through all challenges and triumphs.

It should be readily apparent what the second option entails. Please proceed to the following should you decide to select that option.

The Divine endowments of the metaphysical realm

The utilization of spiritual gifts elevates and empowers one's ministerial endeavors. The agency of the Spirit, operating through bestowed gifts, transmutes the act of engaging in ministry into the essence of being ministers. Christian believers are commonly urged to actualize their purpose through the exploration of their divine endowments; nonetheless, authors such as Warren expound upon how the inclinations of such believers are molded by their spiritual gifts, individuality, life experiences, and aptitudes.

Warren does not undermine the notion of God's empowerment through gifting. Nevertheless, he advises against the imprudent utilization or evaluation of it. The Church requires astute implementation of any instruction pertaining to spiritual gifts.

The Church's comprehension and instruction regarding spiritual gifts is shaped by the doctrinal influence of the teachings delivered by the Apostle Paul. The main catalogues and substantial insights provided by Paul regarding spiritual gifts can be located within the verses Romans 12:3-8, 1 Corinthians 12:1-13:1, and Ephesians 4:7-16. Additional compilations of the New Testament can be ascertained from the verses 1 Peter 4:10-11 and 5:1-7.

Paul's teachings yield overarching principles concerning gifts that can be derived. The composition of the Christ body encompasses diverse individuals endowed with a multitude of talents (1 Corinthians). 12:14). Individuals hold distinct responsibilities within the corpus of believers (Rom. 12:4-5). The roles and obligations of adherents are ascertained and delineated by the endowments (Romans. 12:6). The bestowed blessings shall vary, yet they collectively constitute integral components of the unified entity and are bestowed by the identical Divine force, ultimately serving the shared advantage of the collective entity representing Christ (1 Corinthians). 12:4-7). Every component should contribute to the entirety of the whole (Ephesians). 4:12-13). Each component should demonstrate a shared concern and equal consideration for one another (1 Corinthians 12:25).

The ultimate aim of attaining the complete fulfillment and intended goal set forth by Christ shall be accomplished as every component of the collective entity makes its respective contribution (Ephesians). 4:12-13). The allocation of responsibilities within the Ministry should be determined by an individual's spiritual talents. When Christians actively apply their unique talents and abilities, they tend to depend less on their personal efforts and more on the indwelling strength of the Holy Spirit, thereby enabling ordinary individuals to achieve remarkable outcomes. An individual endowed with the attribute of leadership and given the chance to assume a position of authority will fulfill the divine objectives established by God.

Leadership is an innate quality bestowed upon individuals by a divine power. Apostle Paul explicitly enumerates the quality of leadership in Romans 12:8. The term proistamenos in Greek, as employed by Paul in the book of Romans 12:8, has been rendered as leadership in the New International Version (NIV) translation. The term "the one standing in front" can be interpreted to signify an individual occupying a position of prominence or leadership (Earle 200). The Greek root can be identified as proistemi. It conveys the role of a mariner positioned at the prow of a vessel, directing the course towards a specified location and safeguarding the captain against perils encountered en route (Bryant 108). Christian leaders exercise their leadership by providing guidance, instruction, empowerment, and oversight to the body of Christ in order to effectively carry out its mission and envision.

ONE

Your Initial Role

sets them apart or distinguishes them from others in their industry.

sets them apart, renders them distinctive and noteworthy

irrespective of its multinational or scale, regardless of its size.

Regardless of their impact or potential for profit, whether they are small teams or not,

Established a large and well-coordinated team, implemented rigorous standards, and articulated a clear vision and set of values. Each

Business possesses inherent distinctive attributes.

Nevertheless, if there is something that each and every business possesses

Typically, it refers to effective leadership; an individual who possesses the ability to establish connections and foster meaningful relationships.

by delving into the intricacies of the business beyond what is ordinarily observed

Individual, an individual who possesses a profound comprehension of the business's imperatives, an individual whose personal principles and aspirations are harmonious with those of the organization,

organizational perspective.

Assuming a leadership role within an organization entails a significant amount more than

being an individual possessing the authority to issue commands, or simply

Oversee the operations of a company or organization. It

requires taking on the role of a motivator

Breathing, protector, chief executive officer, and supervisor

Herding a collective of individuals and directing them towards the attainment of objectives, intended results, and a predetermined collection of

beneficial values that contribute to the organization's advancement, as well as the

team.

Conventional wisdom held that a leader was regarded as a type of commander.

supervisor who was observed by all from a position of great prominence

possesses wisdom and expertise; who issues instructions

without eliciting inquiries and ensures its implementation

Through avoiding direct involvement and failing to adhere to their regulations, individuals frequently face justifiable consequences

consequences.

However, circumstances and epochs have undergone a transformation, and alongside

in light of these findings, the advancement and evolution in viewpoint regarding

to whom the responsibility of leadership is assigned. Beyond command and

The implementation of rules and regulations, in addition to the contemporary understanding of leadership, is present

expanded to include the role of an individual who identifies potential opportunities

that contribute to the organization's success and foster an

facilitating a conducive environment for the expansion and progress

Facilitate the acquisition of fresh skills and talent, and guarantee their active and meaningful contribution.

dedicated to advancing the mission of the organization.

Accomplishing this is always a daunting undertaking as it involves much more than

an elaborate puzzle that will require seamless integration

to cultivate an atmosphere conducive to progress by means of

upholding foundational principles, guaranteeing a positive demeanor towards

Engaging in diligent efforts and ensuring that each team member assumes responsibility for the assigned tasks, while adhering to a disciplined work approach.

They collectively unite in providing assistance to other teams.

A contemporary leader immerses themselves in the same level of involvement as their subordinates.

Individually contributing to the team's efforts with enthusiasm and dedication.

Simultaneously, while offering assistance to the remainder of the team.

What is the significance of vision in the context of leadership?

As previously noted, the primary essence of leadership is

to guide the direction and lead the team within an organization

The leader's attitude towards the attainment of the

organizational vision.

The business's vision represents the desired and envisioned endpoint of

The enterprise that encompasses their desired destination

the future, which constitutes their endeavor each time they engage in any task

Contemplating a course of action or reaching a resolution, which yields motivation.

in order to promote the overall mission and objectives of the organization, its constituent departments, teams, and individuals. The vision is

The factors that influence the decision-making process and strategic priorities of the business. It

may differ across enterprises, as each business

is established for various purposes.

For certain individuals, the objective lies in outperforming competing brands, while for others, the aim is to surpass them.

encompasses expanding internationally and extending our coverage

Subsequent to its existing progress, certain individuals simply desire enhanced visibility and recognition.

Renowned and recognized within its target demographic, desired by some.

Characterized by their ingenuity and contemporary approaches, while others exhibit a genuine desire to contribute.

Individuals from diverse backgrounds and for a multitude of reasons.

However, there is no doubt that regardless of the type of

In order to uphold the organizational vision, it is incumbent upon the leader to guarantee that

All members within the team and the broader organization possess the ability to connect and identify with the matter at hand.

by imparting and cultivating the vision within the core of its employees.

and guarantee that it manifests through the nature of the promotional endeavors

organization gets. It functions as a central hub for the staff, providing assistance in

through the establishment of decision prioritization and the articulation of

their daily, future, and enduring endeavors.

What is the significance of strategy in effective leadership?

Prior to a business being able to expand its reach remotely,

An organized and deliberate course of action must be developed in order to pursue the

attainment of its longstanding objectives. It bears resemblance to a meticulously devised strategy.

that is devised and aimed at strategizing the

the trajectory of the enterprise.

It primarily comprises a compilation of implementable strategies that are

strived to ensure that the vision

statement is followed. A strategic plan directs the leader of a

Establishing a strategic partnership with

staff members, clientele, collaborators, vendors, and

stakeholders. The crux of the professional partnership lies in establishing,

devise and operationalize a strategic plan to benefit the organization

attain success in the market and, above all, to

consumers. A comprehensive plan can be formulated over a prolonged duration.

Temporal interval - on an annual, semiannual, or recent basis

engaged in, as an ongoingendeavor encompassing a broad

diverse group of individuals and emphasizing the importance of conducting experiments and

learning.

A strong connection exists between strategy and motivation. As earlier

It is important to underscore that both strategy and vision play a pivotal role in the overall context.

The chief impetus for the leader, the team, and the individual.

in a business. Yet another crucial requirement to facilitate business operations

leadership is motivation.

This tool primarily serves as a means through which the leader can effectively

Employing, can enhance productivity and guarantee the

achievement of goals. A competent leader should consistently demonstrate a willingness to inspire and motivate each and every individual within the organization.

The organization demonstrates its values, standards, and regulations through their verbal and written communication, behavior, and regulatory framework.

By means of developmental programs, mentoring, and personnel

educational initiatives, constructive criticism, and cognitive assistance.

An additional influential incentive is the use of financial resources.

Gift cards and other forms of intangible incentives in the context of consumer purchases

and rewards.

The concept encompasses remuneration and all other related aspects

that can facilitate the professional growth of staff members and enhance their motivation to perform their duties diligently. By

By engaging in this practice, leaders have the opportunity to harness the enthusiasm, determination, and eagerness to contribute exhibited by their employees.

The Leader Of The Organized Group

In order to attain a high level of organization, it is imperative to approach tasks with a methodical and efficient mindset. It is imperative to acquire an understanding of the distinct, interrelated components comprising a entirety and the precise roles played by each component. A proficient leader is an individual who esteems this intricate equilibrium and possesses the ability to judiciously assign responsibilities to appropriate individuals in order to preserve it.

The characteristic of possessing organizational skills is crucial for virtually any undertaking. A leader who exhibits this quality is capable of preserving mental clarity throughout the implementation of a project due to their comprehensive understanding of the people involved, the methods employed, the locations chosen, and the reasons behind their decisions.

The astute leader possesses knowledge of their own strengths and weaknesses, as well as those of the other team members, in an orderly manner. Irrespective of the magnitude of the workload, this exemplary leader possesses the ability to efficiently allocate and delegate tasks to the appropriate departments. This methodical approach will guarantee exceptional performance and output of utmost quality.

How to Become One:

Maintaining a sense of order and structure in one's life is fundamental to realizing any aspirations one may have. Leaders must possess the ability to proficiently strategize and allocate tasks, thereby ensuring the achievement of collective objectives. Employ these strategies to cultivate and exemplify the qualities of an organized leader:

Respect Diversity. It is imperative to acknowledge that every individual possesses unique talents that can contribute positively to the team, alongside areas of weakness that can be compensated for by leveraging the strengths of other team members. Take heed of the unique contributions each member can bring forth and have faith in their ability to execute tasks with utmost proficiency.

Develop a comprehensive framework of regulations. It is imperative for a leader to ensure comprehensive comprehension among all team members regarding their respective roles and the corresponding expectations placed upon them. It is imperative for all individuals, including the designated leader, to comprehend that their contribution holds equal significance to that of their peers. By establishing clarity in this matter, the team rules will become comprehensible to all participants, resulting in a higher likelihood of their adherence.

Acknowledge and attribute proper credit to those who deserve it. One of the duties of a well-structured leader is to discern the diverse endeavors of every member and recognize their respective contributions. Indeed, while functioning collectively as a team, it is important to acknowledge that individuals within the group possess autonomous thinking capabilities. Every individual desires validation for their endeavors, particularly when it is bestowed upon them by their superior. By bestowing this upon them, you are instilling encouragement for that member to persist in their diligent efforts.

Maintain an organized environment. It is self-evident that as an effective leader, one must demonstrate by example. One can most effectively demonstrate this characteristic by maintaining a tidy and meticulously arranged work environment. These conditions foster efficacy and output as they eliminate the time wasted on rummaging through documents for a singular purpose. At the conclusion of each day, ensure that your workspace is tidied up and all items are returned to their respective locations.

If you encounter difficulties in maintaining an organized state, endeavor to embrace a minimalist approach as an alternative. Remove any superfluous objects and individuals that serve to clutter both your environment and thoughts, leaving only the indispensable elements to command attention. Through the formulation of a concise strategic blueprint, all complexities are effectively resolved and the task at hand becomes more manageable.

Performance Evaluation

The process of appraising staff performance is commonly a source of stress, not only for managers but also for employees. For the employees, this signifies a period during which they will be held accountable for all their instances of negligence and misconduct throughout the year. For the manager, it is a time when he must undertake the unenviable task of meticulously documenting all instances where employees have failed to meet expected standards or have engaged in inappropriate behavior throughout the year. However, what necessitates it to be an unpleasant encounter?

A competent manager has the ability to transform this typically unfavorable yearly event into a positive and effective undertaking by employing the following strategies.

Monitor employee performance.

There exist two exemplary methods for overseeing and assessing employee performance. One approach entails the manager maintaining comprehensive records concerning the performance of each employee, whereas the other approach involves requiring employees to maintain personal records of their own performance throughout the year. As a consequence of inherent human tendencies, the manager's perception will be unduly influenced by the employee's shortcomings, thus overshadowing their accomplishments. Conversely, the employee will tend to view their successes as outweighing their failures. Therefore, it is advisable for both the manager and the employee to maintain a record of the employee's performance throughout the year, as this practice will effectively showcase both their accomplishments and shortcomings.

Emphasize successes.

Management can effectively enhance employee retention by placing emphasis on their achievements instead of highlighting their shortcomings. When examining the broader scope, it becomes apparent that an organization sustains momentum throughout the year as a result of the accomplishments of both individuals and teams. Should the failures of the employees outshine their accomplishments, it would result in a complete stagnation of the organization. This observation remains applicable to the global context at large; the rotation of the world is sustained by the benevolent actions undertaken by the majority of humanity, rather than being influenced by the detrimental actions of a minority. Employees experience a heightened sense of motivation when their achievements are accentuated, thereby fostering a deeper sense of loyalty towards the organization.

Does this imply that the identification of employee failures is not warranted?

Areas of improvement.

Eliminate the utilization of the term "failure" entirely from the lexicon of performance assessment. Instead of using "Substitute," opt for "Replace" for a more formal tone. Additionally, consider rephrasing the sentence as follows: "Opt for using the term 'Areas of improvement' instead, as it carries a more nuanced connotation than 'Failure,' implying that the employee is still in a position to make progress." However, it should be noted that the term "Areas of improvement" suggests that there exist a variety of opportunities for the employee to enhance their performance.

The manager may potentially suggest the employee's participation in a training program, the specifics of which, including the content, duration, and location, will be determined based on the areas the employee requires development in. Following the conclusion of the training, it is imperative for the manager to arrange a feedback session wherein both the employee and the manager will engage in a discussion to assess the employee's acquired knowledge and discern her plans for the implementation of the training components to enhance her work performance. Furthermore, it would be prudent to arrange for the employee to deliver a presentation to her colleagues, elucidating the knowledge and skills she acquired through the training. By doing so, the advantageous impacts of the training program can be effectively disseminated among other employees, without incurring any additional expenses for the company.

One additional measure the manager can adopt to facilitate the enhancement of the employee's performance is to arrange periodic counseling sessions involving both the employee and the manager. During these sessions, the manager can observe the employee's progress and identify the specific areas where the employee faces challenges in carrying out their assigned duties.

Occasionally, there may arise situations wherein, despite the aforementioned efforts, the employee fails to attain the expected standards of improvement. This unequivocally signifies that the employee does not possess the fundamental skills necessary to excel in their assigned role. Therefore, it would be advisable for the manager to suggest reassigning her to a different department, where her skills can be utilized more effectively.

www.ingramcontent.com/pod-product-compliance
Lightning Source LLC
Chambersburg PA
CBHW052136110526
44591CB00012B/1745